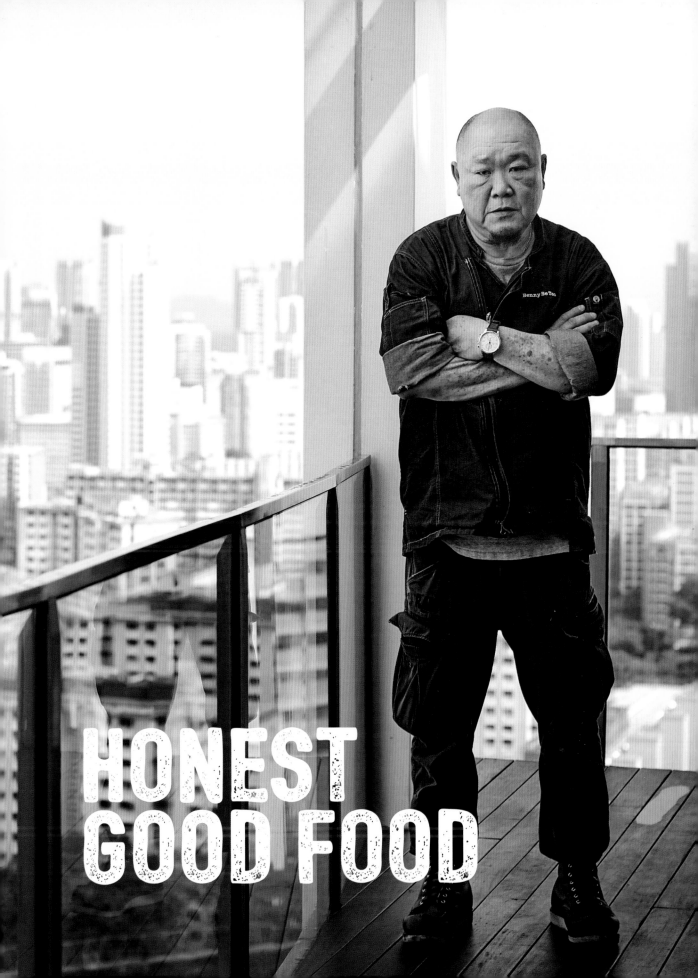

HONEST GOOD FOOD

HONEST GOOD FOOD

CHEF BENNY SE TEO

Bold Flavours, Hearty Eats

mc **Marshall Cavendish**
Cuisine

© 2017 Marshall Cavendish International (Asia) Private Limited

Photography by Ng Chai Soong
Text by Yuling Li

Published by Marshall Cavendish Cuisine
An imprint of Marshall Cavendish International

Other Marshall Cavendish Offices:
Marshall Cavendish Corporation. 99 White Plains Road, Tarrytown NY 10591-9001,
USA • Marshall Cavendish International (Thailand) Co Ltd. 253 Asoke, 12th Flr,
Sukhumvit 21 Road, Klongtoey Nua, Wattana, Bangkok 10110, Thailand • Marshall
Cavendish (Malaysia) Sdn Bhd, Times Subang, Lot 46, Subang Hi-Tech Industrial Park,
Batu Tiga, 40000 Shah Alam, Selangor Darul Ehsan, Malaysia.

Marshall Cavendish is a registered trademark of Times Publishing Limited

National Library Board, Singapore Cataloguing in Publication Data

Name(s): Se Teo, Benny, 1960- | Ng, Chai Soong, photographer. | Li, Yuling, contributor.
Title: Honest good food : bold flavours, hearty eats / chef Benny Se Teo ; photography by
Ng Chai Soong ; text by Yuling Li.
Description: Singapore : Marshall Cavendish Cuisine, [2017]
Identifier(s): OCN 960283897 | ISBN 978-981-47-7102-3
Subject(s): LCSH: Cooking, Singaporean.
Classification: DDC 641.595957–dc23

Printed in Malaysia by TWP Sdn. Bhd.

To my wife Mei,
who has seen me through the tough times

no MATTER
what YOU DO,
YOUR JOB IS TO
tell YOUR STORY.
THROUGH
THIS cookbook,
I tell mine

CONTENTS

SHIOK & SPICY SINGAPOREAN SIGNATURES

ZI CHAR & ASIAN CLASSICS

FUSING FLAVOURS

ABOUT CHEF BENNY SE TEO

WEIGHTS & MEASURES

ACKNOWLEDGEMENTS

To all who have helped in one way or another with this project, thank you! In particular, I would like to thank:

Shirley Lim, for planning my schedule for the numerous photography sessions;

Elf, my marketing manager, for liaising with all the parties involved and for compiling the recipes and photographs;

Chef William, my executive head chef, for making sure the ingredients were there at my disposal for the photography sessions;

Lydia, from Marshall Cavendish, for believing in me and working with me to bring this book to publication;

Yuling, the writer, for being patient with me and sitting through the many sessions, listening to my stories;

Ng Chai Soong, the photographer, for his excellent photography skills;

Andrew Parkinson, my mentor, for guiding me during my internship at Fifteen, London;

Kuik Shiao-Yin, for contributing the two recipes featured in the Ready in Twenty section;

KF Seetoh for his kind words and encouragement;

Ummi Abdullah for unselfishly sharing her Malay cooking techniques with me;

Makcik Maria for her invaluable tips on cooking nasi padang;

And last but not least, my Lord and Saviour Jesus Christ for loving me although I am least lovable.

INTRODUCTION

I love food and I love music. My cooking philosophy is like that of rock music: dare to be different and authentic. This cookbook celebrates both my passions, and I hope to share my story through the recipes that follow.

For those of you who do not know, I am an ex-convict. I struggled with drug addiction in my youth and went in and out of jail because of that. While serving my sentence in prison, I was tea boy to the superintendent, and I cooked for him and the other officers. They didn't complain about the food, so I guess they liked it.

Some years after my release, I joined a disaster-relief project called "Love Turkey". The mission brought medical supplies and other necessities to the victims of the earthquake that struck Turkey in 1999. My role was to run the kitchen and prepare meals for the volunteers from Singapore and Malaysia. Everyone really missed home then, and nothing comforted us more than having a meal consisting of Chinese sausages (*lap cheong*) and curry!

Over the years, friends who have tasted my cooking would often encourage me to go into the food business. Thus in 2005, I started Goshen, my first restaurant. It was a social enterprise that hired ex-offenders. Unfortunately, things did not work out as I had hoped, and Goshen closed its doors in 2006.

That same year, I also found out about Jamie Oliver's Fifteen, a successful non-profit restaurant based in London. I wrote to Liam Black, then CEO of Fifteen, and asked if I could join their apprenticeship programme. I was turned down many times, but I didn't give up trying. I was eventually offered a spot — on condition that I found my own way to London.

Working in the kitchen of Jamie Oliver's Fifteen was an eye-opening and unforgettable experience for me. I learnt so much in just three weeks. The chefs were highly professional and showed a lot of pride in their work. I still remember how a senior corrected me when I tossed a salad with one hand instead of two. The attention to detail, such as using both hands to gently mix a salad, impressed me.

You could say I returned to Singapore a different man. Exactly how different is something I am still discovering today. It was a short but intense stint, and there were many concepts that I did not understand then, which became clearer with time.

In 2007, I co-founded Eighteen Chefs and opened the first outlet at Eastpoint Mall in the east of Singapore. Today, there are more than 12 Eighteen Chefs outlets scattered across the island, a testament that people enjoy eating our food.

What is the secret to making good food, you ask? Let me tell you the honest truth: there is no secret. Cooking, like life, becomes better through trial and error. Of course, if you want some ideas, refer to the recipes in this book! They are meant to be easy to follow, and you will be able to recreate the dishes in your own kitchen.

I have also included tips that I picked up over the years from friends in Singapore and all around the world. On pages 50 and 52, you will find two special recipes contributed by my friend, Kuik Shiao-Yin, who co-founded Food For Thought, a popular local restaurant that is also a social enterprise. I know you will enjoy her recipes too.

At home, I cook with whatever I can find in my fridge and pantry. Should I find that I am out of black vinegar when I want to cook *kung po* chicken, I use balsamic vinegar as a substitute if that is what I have on hand. And why not? Don't get me wrong; I am not saying that anything goes, but cooking should not be restrictive. Work with what you have and you will be surprised by how well a dish can turn out. But should the experiment fail, just try again!

Chef Benny

The Power of an Encouraging Word

When I was young, I knew I was good at replicating dishes, but I never thought of myself as a chef. In 1999, I joined a disaster-relief project called Love Turkey where I was tasked with cooking for the other volunteers who were mostly doctors and nurses. They looked forward to every meal and told me that my cooking helped them feel less homesick. Finally at the age of 39, I started to consider the possibility that I could be a chef (I was a dispatch rider then). Sometimes, people have gifts that they do not know of. Don't underestimate the power of your encouragement to help others realise their gifts.

HOME-STYLE COMFORT FOOD

There is a story behind
every recipe featured in this
book. The dishes in this section
are made of happy, cherished
moments shared with family and
friends around the table.

The Cantonese nickname for this dish is *tai yi ma ka loi,* which literally means "Big Aunt marries off her daughter". My late parents served this dish at their wedding banquet back in Hoiping, their hometown in Guangdong province, China. Back then, it was considered a luxury. My mum's cooking was not fancy, but I enjoyed the simple dishes, like this one, all the same.

HAIRY GOURD WITH GLASS NOODLES AND DRIED PRAWNS

Serves 4–5

INGREDIENTS

500 g (1 lb 1½ oz) hairy gourd
50 g (1¾ oz) glass noodles
50 g (1¾ oz) dried prawns (*hae bee*)
1 Tbsp cooking oil
2 cloves garlic, peeled and chopped
Water, as needed
1 Tbsp sea salt

METHOD

1. Rinse hairy ground and scrape off skin. Halve, then cut into thin strips. Soak glass noodles in water until softened. Set aside. Soak dried prawns in warm water until softened. Drain well and set aside.

2. Heat oil in a pan over medium heat. Add garlic and stir-fry until golden brown. Add dried prawns and stir-fry until fragrant. Add hairy gourd and stir-fry to mix.

3. Add a little water to prevent burning. Continue to braise until hairy gourd is softened. Taste and adjust seasoning with salt.

4. Add glass noodles and enough water to cover half the ingredients. Mix well and simmer for 5 minutes or until glass noodles are softened. Dish out and serve hot as part of a meal.

My late father loved eating roast pork belly (*siew yoke*), especially the fatty part. Enjoy this with English mustard; that's the way it is traditionally eaten and it's also how I serve it at home. This dish can be prepared using a simple oven. Follow the steps carefully and you won't go wrong!

ROAST CRACKLED PORK BELLY (SIEW YOKE)

Serves 4–5

INGREDIENTS

1.4 kg (3 lb 2 oz) pork belly
2 Tbsp sea salt
1 piece red fermented bean curd
2 Tbsp five-spice powder
2 Tbsp Shaoxing wine
White vinegar, as needed
English mustard

METHOD

1. Start preparations a day ahead. Wash and pat dry pork belly. Mix salt, red fermented bean curd, five-spice powder and Shaoxing wine and rub meat thoroughly with this mixture.

2. Puncture pork belly skin with a meat pricker, then brush skin with vinegar. Place pork belly in an uncovered dish and keep refrigerated overnight.

3. When ready to cook, pre-heat oven to 200°C (400°F).

4. Pierce pork belly diagonally across using 2 metal skewers to keep meat flat while roasting. Place on a baking tray in the middle rack of oven. Lower oven temperature to 180°C (350°F).

5. Roast for about 40 minutes, then remove from oven. Brush skin with vinegar and puncture with the meat pricker again.

6. Increase oven temperature to 200°C and continue to roast until skin is blistered and charred. Remove pork from oven and use a serrated knife to scrape away charred bits. Leave meat to rest for about 30 minutes.

7. Remove skewers and slice. Serve pork with mustard. Enjoy as part of a meal or with white rice.

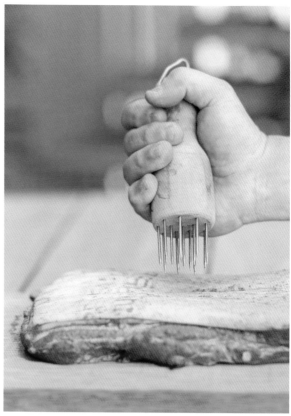

This is an unforgettable dish that my late mother used to prepare for me. I remember when I was detained at the police station for using drugs, and Mum had come to bail me out. It was late and I had not eaten. When we got home, she used whatever she had in the fridge, and prepared this dish in the rice cooker. All it took was a few minutes. I remember thinking that there was no better taste on earth than this.

STEAMED PORK BELLY WITH **PRAWN PASTE SAUCE**

Serves 2–3

INGREDIENTS

200 g (7 oz) pork belly
¾ Tbsp fine shrimp paste
1 tsp cooking oil
1½ tsp ground white pepper
2 tsp sugar
1 tsp cornflour
2 Tbsp water
1 red chilli, sliced
1 spring onion (scallion), sliced

METHOD

1. Cut pork belly into slices. Place on a steaming plate and add fine shrimp paste, oil, pepper, sugar, cornflour and water. Mix well, cover and set aside to marinate for 30 minutes.

2. Place in a steamer over rapidly boiling water and steam for 10 minutes or until pork well cooked.

3. Garnish with red chillies and spring onion. Serve hot as part of a meal or with white rice.

At my home, nothing goes to waste. You'll be surprised at the delicious dishes that can be made from leftovers. Whether it's leftover chicken, roast pork or duck, all you need is to caramelize it with dark soy sauce to turn it into an appetising stir-fry.

LEFTOVER MAGIC

Serves 4–5

INGREDIENTS

2 Tbsp cooking oil
4 cloves garlic, peeled
  and sliced
500 g (1 lb 1½ oz) leftover
  steamed chicken, roast duck
  and/or roast pork (*siew yoke*)
2 Tbsp dark soy sauce
2 Tbsp sugar
3 spring onions (scallions),
  cut into short lengths

METHOD

1. Heat oil in a pan over medium heat. Add garlic and stir-fry until fragrant. Add leftovers and mix well.

2. Add dark soy sauce, sugar and spring onions. Mix well and continue to stir-fry until caramelized.

3. Dish out and serve as part of a meal or with white rice.

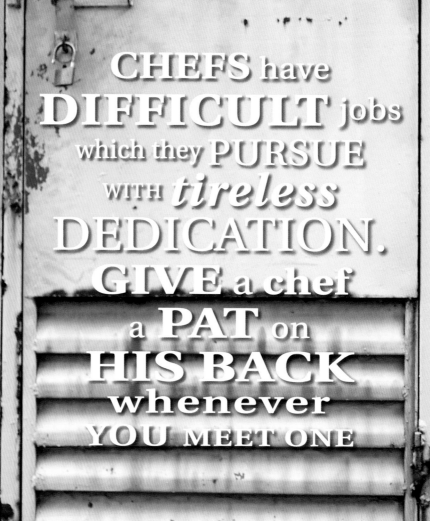

CHEFS have **DIFFICULT** jobs which they **PURSUE** WITH *tireless* **DEDICATION.** **GIVE** a chef a **PAT** on **HIS BACK** whenever **YOU** MEET ONE

Who says you can't make Chinese BBQ pork (*char siew*)
using a pan on the stovetop? You don't need an industrial grade
oven to get it nice and caramelised. Let me show you how it's done.
I promise it will taste every bit as good as it looks.

PAN-ROASTED CHINESE BBQ PORK (CHAR SIEW)

Serves 4–5

INGREDIENTS

400 g (14⅓ oz) pork shoulder
2 Tbsp maltose
1 Tbsp sugar
6 Tbsp hot water

SAUCE

1 tsp red food colouring
½ Tbsp fermented bean paste, minced
1 cube red fermented bean curd

4 Tbsp hoisin sauce
6 Tbsp Chinese rose wine
1 Tbsp sesame paste
1 tsp maltose
4 Tbsp sugar
2 Tbsp light soy sauce
1 Tbsp dark soy sauce
125 ml (4 fl oz / ½ cup) water

METHOD

1. Combine ingredients for sauce in a bowl. Add pork and coat
well. Cover and place in the refrigerator to marinate overnight.

2. Place marinated pork together with sauce in a deep saucepan.
Bring sauce to a boil over high heat, then lower heat and simmer
until pork is tender, turning pork over occasionally as it cooks.
This will take 45–60 minutes.

3. When pork is tender, remove from pan and set aside.
Continue to simmer sauce until thick and syrupy. Set aside
to serve with pork.

4. Combine maltose, sugar and hot water in a bowl. Heat a
non-stick pan over medium heat. Add maltose mixture and
stir until it starts to brown. Add pork and coat well. Leave
to caramelise until skin is well-charred or as desired.

5. Remove pork from pan. Set aside for about 5 minutes before
slicing. Drizzle pork with sauce. Serve as part of a meal or with
white rice.

This dish is also known as *ter ka bee hoon*. It is a Hokkien staple that I love. Canned pork trotters are a must. If you plan to add fresh meat, go for the front trotters – they're much meatier than the hind.

RICE VERMICELLI WITH PORK TROTTERS

Serves 4–5

INGREDIENTS

200 g (7 oz) dried rice vermicelli (*bee hoon*)
1 large can (397 g / 13¼ oz) braised pork trotters with mushrooms
1 Tbsp pork lard, as needed
70 g (2½ oz) bean sprouts
1 tsp sugar
1 Tbsp light soy sauce
1 tsp dark soy sauce
1 tsp chicken seasoning powder
15 g (½ oz) fried shallots
1 spring onion (scallion), chopped

METHOD

1. Soak rice vermicelli in water for 20 minutes until softened. Drain well. Skim off excess oil from braised pork leg.

2. Heat pork lard in a pan over medium heat. Add bean sprouts and stir-fry lightly. Add 3 Tbsp stock from canned pork trotters, sugar, light soy sauce and dark soy sauce. Mix well.

3. Add rice vermicelli and stir-fry for about 1 minute. Add chicken seasoning powder and braised pork trotters with mushrooms. Cover pan with a lid and let cook over high heat for about 10 minutes.

4. Stir in fried shallots and chopped spring onion. Dish out and serve.

Century eggs are often associated with congee, but I've found that they also go very well with noodles. This is a classic example of simple, comfort food made out of desperation — using whatever is in the pantry. When you're hungry, you can cook up something really tasty with just a little creativity.

BEE TAI MAK WITH CENTURY EGG

Serves 2

INGREDIENTS

3 Tbsp cooking oil

2 shallots, peeled and sliced

2 cloves garlic, peeled and sliced

50 g (1¾ oz) preserved sweet turnip (*teem chye poh*), chopped

250 g (9 oz) short rice noodles (*bee tai mak*)

1 Tbsp abalone bouillon

1 tsp light soy sauce

50 g (1¾ oz) bean sprouts

2 century eggs, peeled and cut into cubes

1 Tbsp fried pork lard

1 spring onion (scallion), chopped

METHOD

1. Heat oil in a pan over medium heat. Add shallots, garlic and preserved sweet turnip and stir-fry until fragrant.

2. Add short rice noodles, abalone bouillon and light soy sauce and stir-fry lightly.

3. Add bean sprouts and century eggs and stir-fry until bean sprouts are lightly cooked.

4. Dish out and top with fried pork lard and chopped spring onion. Serve.

You either love this dish or hate it. And I love it. Why do I love it?
Because it has a lot of fat! This is a super comfort food that melts in the mouth.

BRAISED PORK BUNS
(KONG BAK PAU)

Serves 4–6

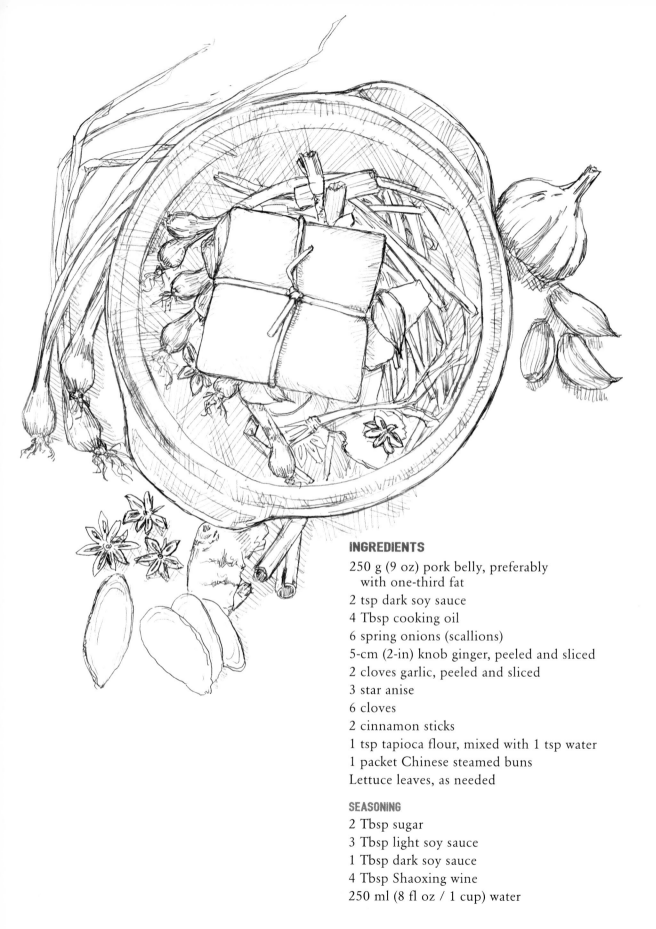

INGREDIENTS

250 g (9 oz) pork belly, preferably
  with one-third fat

2 tsp dark soy sauce

4 Tbsp cooking oil

6 spring onions (scallions)

5-cm (2-in) knob ginger, peeled and sliced

2 cloves garlic, peeled and sliced

3 star anise

6 cloves

2 cinnamon sticks

1 tsp tapioca flour, mixed with 1 tsp water

1 packet Chinese steamed buns

Lettuce leaves, as needed

SEASONING

2 Tbsp sugar

3 Tbsp light soy sauce

1 Tbsp dark soy sauce

4 Tbsp Shaoxing wine

250 ml (8 fl oz / 1 cup) water

METHOD

1. Boil a pot of water and blanch pork belly to remove any impurities. Drain and pat dry. Rub pork belly skin with 1 tsp dark soy sauce.

2. Heat oil in a large pan over medium heat. Place pork belly carefully into pan. Increase to medium-high heat to allow pork belly skin to crisp up in oil. When skin is evenly browned and crisp, turn off heat and remove pork. Drain excess oil and set aside. Allow pork belly to cool slightly before tying with butcher string to help retain shape of pork belly.

3. Place spring onions, ginger, garlic, star anise, cloves and cinnamon sticks in a clay pot. Place pork belly over ingredients, skin side down. Add seasoning and braise over low heat for 1 hour. Turn pork belly over and braise for another 1 hour until pork is tender. Remove and cut into thin slices.

4. Add tapioca flour slurry to braising sauce and simmer over low heat to thicken sauce.

5. Steam Chinese buns. To serve, make a sandwich with Chinese buns, lettuce leaves and braised pork belly. Drizzle with sauce.

There are two schools of thought about how Hainanese pork chops should be done. One says the meat should be very thick. The other says it should be crispy, like deep-fried crackers (*keropok*). I'm with the second. The secret to crispy pork chops is to slice the meat thinly and hammer it with a meat mallet before breading. The other secret is saltine crackers (*soda piah*).

HAINANESE PORK CHOP

Serves 4–5

INGREDIENTS

5 slices pork loin, each about 100 g (3½ oz)
Cooking oil, as needed
1 large potato, peeled and cut into wedges
3 eggs, beaten
8 saltine crackers, finely crushed
1 Tbsp butter
2 Tbsp green peas
3 cherry tomatoes, halved
1 medium red onion, peeled and sliced

MARINADE

1 Tbsp light soy sauce
½ Tbsp sugar
½ Tbsp sesame oil
1 tsp tapioca flour
A dash of ground white pepper

SAUCE

2 Tbsp tomato ketchup
1 Tbsp sugar
1 tsp light soy sauce
1 tsp chicken seasoning powder
1 Tbsp plain flour
125 ml (4 fl oz / ½ cup) water

METHOD

1. Using a meat tenderizer, pound pork until tender. Combine ingredients for marinade in a bowl. Add pork and mix well. Cover and set aside to marinate for 1 hour.

2. Heat 2 Tbsp oil in a pan over medium heat. Add potato wedges and cook until golden brown on all sides. Remove and set aside.

3. Heat sufficient oil for deep-frying in a pan over medium heat.

4. Dip marinated pork in beaten egg, then coat with crushed cream crackers. Repeat this step twice.

5. Place pork gently into hot oil and deep-fry until golden brown and crispy. Set aside to drain.

6. Heat 2 Tbsp oil and butter in a clean pan over medium heat. Combine ingredients for sauce in a bowl and add to pan. Bring to the boil, then add green peas, tomatoes, onion and potato wedges. Cook for 1–2 minutes.

7. Slice pork into thick strips and arrange on a serving plate. Ladle sauce over. Serve as part of a meal or with white rice.

I first heard about Benny and his restaurant, Goshen, from my church which had been heavily involved in the prison ministry. However, Goshen closed down before I had the chance to eat there. Despite that, I was encouraged to hear from friends how Benny persisted to start Eighteen Chefs and push it through a period of near failure to get it to the great success it is today. It was only years later at a public talk that I would hear him share how desperate and dark a time it was for him then, that I got to know him personally.

In the Bible, Goshen is a desert area where nothing could grow, but God still used it to grow good things for generations to come. Benny's life and the food he cooks tell us a story that even the simple can be made superb, the humble can be made whole and that everyone can choose to taste the good life.

Kuik Shiao-Yin
Director, The Thought Collective

HOME-STYLE COMFORT FOOD: READY IN TWENTY

The following two recipes are contributed by Kuik Shiao-Yin, co-founder of The Thought Collective, a social enterprise. I met Shiao-Yin several years ago at an F&B trade show, and she later invited me to speak to a group of aspiring restaurant owners at Food for Thought. One day, over coffee at The Black Seed, I asked Shiao-Yin if she would like to contribute recipes to my cookbook. She gamely agreed, so here are her favourite quick and fuss-free home-cooked meals — perfect for busy working mothers like Shiao-Yin.

Shiao-Yin's mother used to make this for her family, before canned food became classified as unhealthy. One of Shiao-Yin's favourite comfort foods, this Singapore-style corned beef hash includes sliced spicy red chillies for an extra kick.

CORNED BEEF HASH

Serves 4–5

INGREDIENTS

2 medium potatoes, peeled and diced
Salt, as needed
1 Tbsp cooking oil
1 large red onion, peeled and diced
1 can (340 g / 12 oz) corned beef, mashed
2 red chillies, sliced
Ground black pepper, to taste
1 sprig coriander leaves (cilantro), chopped

METHOD

1. Place potatoes in a large pot and cover with water. Add a large pinch of salt and bring to a boil. Cook over moderately high heat until potatoes are tender. Drain and set aside.

2. Heat oil in a large non-stick pan over medium heat. Add onion and cook until onion is just starting to soften. Stir in potatoes and corned beef. Season with black pepper. Mix evenly, then flatten slightly with a spatula.

3. Dish out and garnish with chillies and coriander. Serve with bread.

"This is a humble dish which you can easily 'dress up' with some good bread."

~ Shiao-Yin

After work, Shiao-Yin is usually too tired to cook anything fancy. This simple and tasty dish is what she calls a good "TV dinner", using simple ingredients commonly stocked by Singaporean households. It's put together like a pasta dish: prepare the noodles and meat sauce separately, then mix them together before serving.

ASIAN 'PASTA' (KWAY TEOW WITH MINCED MEAT SAUCE)

Serves 4–5

INGREDIENTS

300 g (11 oz) minced pork
1 Tbsp light soy sauce
1 Tbsp sesame oil
A dash of ground white pepper
420 g (14 oz) thin flat rice noodles (Ipoh *hor fun*)
1 Tbsp cooking oil
3 cloves garlic, peeled and chopped
2–3 fish cakes, sliced
100 g (3½ oz) bean sprouts
Water, as needed
1 red chilli, sliced
1 Tbsp fried shallots
1 Tbsp crispy silver fish
1 sprig coriander leaves (cilantro), chopped

METHOD

1. Season minced pork with light soy sauce, sesame oil and white pepper. Mix well and set aside for 10–15 minutes.

2. Blanch noodles in a pot of boiling water. Drain and set aside.

3. Heat oil in a wok over medium heat. Add garlic and stir-fry until fragrant. Add minced pork and stir-fry until meat is cooked through.

4. Add fish cakes and bean sprouts. Mix well. Add some water and continue to cook until bean sprouts are lightly cooked.

5. Stir in noodles and mix well. Dish out and garnish with chilli, fried shallots, crispy silver fish and coriander leaves. Serve.

SHIOK & SPICY SINGAPOREAN SIGNATURES

I am proud to be
a Singaporean. Our cuisine
is known around the world.
People may not know
much about our country,
but they would definitely
have heard of our food.

There are two steps you cannot skip if you want to make very good chicken rice.
For tender meat, immerse the chicken in iced water after boiling.
To make the rice extra fragrant, fry the shallots and garlic in chicken fat.

HAINANESE CHICKEN RICE

Serves 6–8

INGREDIENTS

CHICKEN

Water, as needed

2 Tbsp salt

15 g (½ oz) sliced ginger

5 cloves garlic, peeled and sliced

4 pandan leaves, cleaned
and knotted

2 kg (4 lb 6 oz) chicken

Iced water

Sesame oil, as needed

CHICKEN OIL

3 Tbsp cooking oil

15 g (½ oz) chicken fat

1 shallot, peeled and sliced

5 g (⅙ oz) sliced ginger

2 cloves garlic, peeled, chopped

RICE

1 kg (2 lb 3 oz) jasmine rice

4 Tbsp chicken oil

2 shallots, peeled

3 cloves garlic, peeled, chopped

20 g (⅔ oz) sliced ginger

1½ tsp chicken seasoning
powder

1½ tsp salt

6 pandan leaves, cleaned
and knotted

CHILLI SAUCE

60 g (2¼ oz) red chillies,
chopped

90 g (3¼ oz) bird's eye chillies,
chopped

50 g (1¾ oz) ginger, peeled
and sliced

50 g (1¾ oz) garlic, peeled

2 Tbsp sugar

1 tsp salt

½ tsp chicken seasoning
powder

Juice from 150 g (5⅓ oz)
calamansi limes

1 tsp chicken oil

1 Tbsp sesame oil

DRESSING

2 Tbsp light soy sauce

2 Tbsp sesame oil

1 tsp chicken seasoning powder

4 Tbsp chicken broth

GARNISH

1 medium cucumber, sliced

2 medium tomatoes, sliced

1 sprig coriander leaves
(cilantro), cut into short
lengths

1 spring onion (scallion),
cut into thin strips

1 red chilli, cut into long,
thin strips

TIP Choose a bird that weighs
2 kg (4 lb 6 oz) or more,
and ask the butcher for extra
chicken fat that you can use
in preparing the rice.

NOTE This chilli sauce is also
used in the chilli crab recipe
on page 80. The sauce will
keep for up to 3 months in
the freezer.

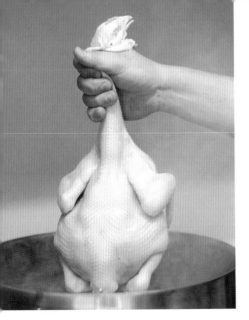

METHOD

1. Prepare chicken. Bring water, salt, ginger, garlic and pandan leaf to a boil in a large stockpot. When water is boiling, hang chicken on a chicken hook. Lower chicken into boiling water, then lift it up. Repeat twice. Submerge chicken, breast side down in boiling water. Turn to low heat and simmer, partially covered for 40 minutes.

2. Remove chicken and place in a large pot of iced water for 15 minutes. Rub chicken with sesame oil and chop to serve. Reserve chicken broth for later use.

3. Prepare chicken oil. Heat oil in a pan over medium heat. Add chicken fat, shallot, ginger and garlic and fry until chicken fat is golden brown and crisp. Measure 4 Tbsp oil for cooking rice (and 1 tsp for chilli sauce) and discard crispy chicken fat.

4. Prepare rice. Wash rice and soak for 30 minutes. Drain well. Heat chicken oil in a large saucepan over medium heat. Fry shallots, garlic and ginger until golden brown. Add rice and stir-fry for about 10 minutes until fragrant. Transfer rice to a rice cooker. Add 1 litre (32 fl oz / 4 cups) chicken broth, chicken seasoning powder and salt. Add pandan leaves and turn on rice cooker to cook rice.

5. Prepare chilli sauce. Using a food processor, process chillies, ginger, garlic, sugar, salt and chicken seasoning powder until fine. Add calamansi juice, chicken oil and sesame oil. Mix well.

6. Combine all ingredients for dressing and mix well.

7. To serve, line a serving plate with cucumber and tomato slices. Arrange chicken on top. Pour dressing over chicken and garnish with coriander and spring onion. Serve with chicken rice, chilli sauce and dark soy sauce.

Of my happy childhood days, I will always remember eating the curry that my Indian neighbour would often prepare. There are many ways of cooking curry, and the first version I learnt to make was Indian. The Chinese way of cooking curry is more methodical, with different ingredients introduced in separate batches. The Indian style focuses on the slow stewing process. Over the years, my style has become something in between.

INDIAN-CHINESE CHICKEN CURRY

Serves 4–5

INGREDIENTS

1 kg (2 lb 3 oz) chicken
3 medium potatoes, peeled

MARINADE

4-cm (1½-in) ginger, peeled and sliced
6 cloves garlic, peeled
200 g (7 oz) store-bought chilli paste (*cili boh*)
1 Tbsp turmeric powder
4 Tbsp meat curry powder
1 tsp chicken seasoning powder
2 Tbsp salt
2 tsp sugar
A dollop of yoghurt
1 can (390 g / 13 oz) evaporated milk
2 green chillies, seeded and halved
1 cinnamon stick
2 star anise
6 cloves
12 cardamom pods
20 g (⅔ oz) cashew nuts, ground
25 g (⅘ oz) fried shallots
1 large tomato, cut into wedges
3 stalks curry leaves
2 sprigs coriander leaves (cilantro), finely chopped

METHOD

1. Clean and cut chicken into 6–8 pieces.

2. Pound ginger and garlic into a paste. Transfer to a large bowl and mix well with chilli paste, turmeric powder, meat curry powder, chicken seasoning powder, salt, sugar, yoghurt and evaporated milk. Add remaining ingredients for marinade to bowl, then add chicken and mix well. Transfer to a saucepan. Cook over low heat for 30 minutes or until oil separates.

3. Boil a pot of water and cook potatoes until tender. Drain potatoes and cut into large pieces. Add to curry and mix well.

4. Serve hot with white rice or bread.

My Eurasian friends introduced this dish to me. Commonly cooked on Boxing Day, Devil Curry combines Christmas leftovers, like cocktail sausages, ham, cabbage and even roasted pork (*siew yoke*) with chilli paste (*cili boh*), white vinegar, mustard seeds and mustard.

DEVIL CURRY

Serves 4–5

INGREDIENTS

5 Tbsp cooking oil

4 heaped Tbsp store-bought chilli paste (*cili boh*)

1 Tbsp mustard seeds

500 g (1 lb 1½ oz) cooked chicken, cocktail sausages and/or roast pork (*siew yoke*)

1 carrot, peeled and cut into chunks

2 baby corn cobs, halved

1 Tbsp English mustard

2 tsp white vinegar

2 tsp chicken seasoning powder

1 Tbsp sea salt

½ Tbsp sugar

Water, as needed

1 Tbsp tomato ketchup

SPICE PASTE

2 medium red onions, peeled and sliced

5-cm (2-in) knob ginger, peeled and sliced

4 dried chillies, seeds discarded and soaked to soften

6 cloves garlic, peeled and sliced

5 candlenuts

GARNISH

1 spring onion (scallion), cut into 5-cm (2-in) lengths

A handful of coriander leaves (cilantro), chopped

2–3 bird's eye chillies

METHOD

1. Using a food processor, process all ingredients for spice paste into a paste. Heat oil in a large saucepan over medium heat. Add spice paste and chilli paste and stir-fry until fragrant.

2. Add mustard seeds and mix well. Add chicken, sausages and/or roasted pork, carrot and baby corn. Mix to coat ingredients with paste.

3. Add mustard, vinegar, chicken seasoning powder, salt and sugar. Add sufficient water to cover ingredients. Turn heat to low and simmer for 20–25 minutes. Skim off any excess oil on the surface. Stir in tomato ketchup.

4. Garnish with spring onions, coriander leaves and bird's eye chillies before serving.

basically,
I'M AFRAID *of*
everything
IN LIFE... *except*
EATING

When I was a boy, I ran freely around my neighbourhood and often visited
my Indian friend's home. I would ask my friend's mother about the spices
she used in her cooking. Then I would return home and ask my mum for some money
so that I could buy the ingredients and try making the dishes myself.
This curry reminds me of the good old days, and is fantastic with roti prata.

LAMB LENTIL CURRY

Serves 4–5

INGREDIENTS

100 g (3½ oz) split lentils

700 g (1½ lb) lamb ribs

2 Tbsp cooking oil

1 medium red onion, peeled
and chopped

1 cinnamon stick

1 Tbsp mustard seeds

15 cardamom pods

15 cloves

1 bay leaf

2 stalks curry leaves

5 Tbsp tamarind water

100 ml (3½ fl oz) coconut milk

1½ Tbsp salt

1 Tbsp sugar

2 tsp lamb bouillon

1 medium carrot, peeled
and cut into chunks

1 medium potato, peeled
and cut into quarters

1 medium aubergine (eggplant),
sliced

Ghee, to taste

SPICE PASTE

5-cm (2-in) knob ginger,
peeled and sliced

8 cloves garlic, peeled and
sliced

50 g (1¾ oz) cashew nuts

3 green chillies

2 Tbsp meat curry powder

1 Tbsp turmeric powder

METHOD

1. Soak lentils in water for 30 minutes, then drain. Using a
food processor, process lentils slightly. Blanch lamb ribs in
boiling water and drain.

2. Half-fill a large stockpot with water and add lamb ribs
and lentils. Bring to the boil.

3. Using a food processor, process all ingredients for
spice paste into a paste. Heat 2 Tbsp oil in a pan over
medium heat. Add spice paste, red onion, cinnamon,
mustard seeds, cardamom, cloves and bay leaf and stir-fry
until aromatic. Add mixture to stockpot.

4. Add curry leaves, tamarind water, coconut milk, salt,
sugar and lamb bouillon. Cover pot with lid and cook,
stirring regularly to prevent mixture from sticking and
burning.

5. Add carrot, potato and aubergine. Lower heat and
simmer until lamb is tender. Stir in some ghee for flavour.
Serve as part of a meal.

TIP Like risotto, lentils require constant stirring to
prevent burning. As a shortcut, I buy split lentils that
cook faster. I also presoak the lentils and run them
through a blender.

Good beef *rendang* is tender and fragrant with sweet, spicy and smoky flavours. You can smell my *rendang* cooking from doors away because I use turmeric leaves and kaffir lime. The star ingredient in my *rendang* is ground toasted coconut (*kerisek*), which I discovered recently, thanks to Ummi Abdullah, a fellow chef and friend. She was very kind to invite me into her kitchen to observe her making the dish from scratch. She also explained the different steps of preparing the perfect beef *rendang*. Till today, I am still impressed by how spotlessly clean her kitchen is!

BEEF RENDANG

Serves 6–8

INGREDIENTS

2 cinnamon sticks

2 star anise

1½ Tbsp fried shallots

7 cardamom pods

1 kg (2 lb 3 oz) beef shin, cut into cubes

200 ml (6⅔ fl oz) coconut milk

500 ml (16 fl oz / 2 cups) water + more as needed

Cooking oil

SPICE PASTE

25 g (⅘ oz) candlenuts

60 g (2¼ oz) chicken seasoning powder

15 g (½ oz) galangal, peeled and sliced

85 g (2⅘ oz) ground toasted coconut (*kerisek*)

420 g (14 oz) large red onions, peeled and sliced

1 stalk lemongrass, ends trimmed and bruised

10 kaffir lime leaves

60 g (2¼ oz) meat curry powder

90 g (3 oz) red chillies

140 g (4⅔ oz) *rendang* paste

70 g (2½ oz) sugar

1 turmeric leaf

10 g (⅓ oz) turmeric, peeled and sliced

METHOD

1. Using a food processor, process all ingredients for spice paste into a paste. Heat oil in a stockpot over medium heat. Add spice paste, cinnamon, star anise, fried shallots and cardamoms and stir-fry until aromatic.

2. Add beef and stir-fry for 2 minutes. Add coconut milk and water and simmer over medium heat, stirring frequently until meat is almost fully cooked through. Top up with more water as needed.

3. Lower heat and simmer for about 3 hours until meat is tender and gravy is thick and reduced. Dish out and serve as part of a meal.

NOTE Ground toasted coconut (*kerisek*) is available from some stalls in the market. To make your own, purchase freshly grated mature coconut and toast in a dry non-stick pan over low or medium heat, stirring constantly until golden brown. Set aside to cool before pounding or blending until fine. Store any excess in the freezer.

You won't find this at every Malay nasi padang stall although it is very popular. Typically served on festive occasions, *ayam masak merah* can be troublesome to make with the many ingredients and steps involved. What makes this dish so special is the combination of spicy *sambal*, tangy tomato paste and crispy shallots. Every bite is an explosion of sensations in your mouth.

AYAM MASAK MERAH

Serves 3–4

INGREDIENTS

Cooking oil, as needed
2 chicken drumsticks,
    each cut into 3 pieces
3 Tbsp tomato ketchup
1 tomato, diced
3 Tbsp fried shallots
250 ml (8 fl oz / 1 cup) water
8 baby carrots
1 large red onion, peeled
    and cut into rings
1 sprig coriander leaves
    (cilantro), chopped
Boiled green peas, as desired

SAMBAL TUMIS

160 g (5⅓ oz) large red onion,
    peeled and sliced
30 g (1 oz) dried chillies, seeds
    discarded and soaked to soften
30 g (1 oz) red chillies
15 g (½ oz) red bird's eye chillies
10 g (⅓ oz) garlic, peeled
10 g (⅓ oz) dried prawn paste
    (*belacan*), toasted
180 g (6 oz) store-bought
    chilli paste (*cili boh*)
6 g (⅕ oz) tamarind paste, mixed
    with 4 Tbsp water and strained
1 tsp chicken seasoning powder
30 g (1 oz) sugar

METHOD

1. Using a food processor, process all ingredients for *sambal tumis* into a paste.

2. Heat 2 Tbsp oil in a deep pan or pot over medium heat. Add chicken and fry until chicken is brown. Add *sambal tumis*, tomato ketchup, diced tomato, fried shallots and water. Simmer over medium heat for 20 minutes.

3. Add baby carrots and simmer for another 10 minutes.

4. Dish out and top with onion, coriander leaves and green peas. Serve as part of a meal.

In my opinion, the best *sambal* cuttlefish in Singapore is from the Marine Terrace market. For nearly two decades, I have frequented the same stall, so it is fitting that I include a recipe inspired by their special dish.

SAMBAL TUMIS CUTTLEFISH

Serves 3–4

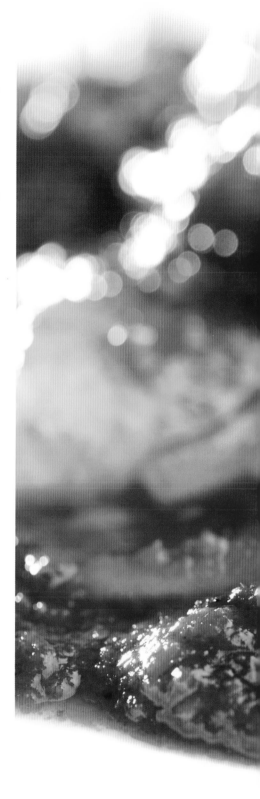

INGREDIENTS

Cooking oil, as needed
300 g (11 oz) cuttlefish, sliced
120 g (4 oz) sugar
300 g (11 oz) tomato ketchup
4 Tbsp water

SAMBAL TUMIS

90 g (3 oz) large red onion, peeled and sliced
15 g (½ oz) dried chillies, seeds discarded and soaked to soften
15 g (½ oz) red chillies
10 g (⅓ oz) red bird's eye chillies
6 g (⅕ oz) garlic, peeled
5 g (⅙ oz) dried prawn paste (*belacan*), toasted
110 g (3⅔ oz) store-bought chilli paste (*cili boh*)
3 g (¹⁄₁₀ oz) tamarind paste, mixed with 2 Tbsp water and strained
8 g (¼ oz) chicken seasoning powder
20 g (⅔ oz) sugar

METHOD

1. Using a food processor, process all ingredients for *sambal tumis* into a paste. Heat 2 Tbsp oil in a pan over medium heat. Add spice paste and stir-fry until paste separates from oil.

2. Add cuttlefish, sugar, tomato ketchup and water. Lower heat and simmer for 20 minutes or until cuttlefish is tender and gravy is thickened.

3. Dish out and serve as part of a meal.

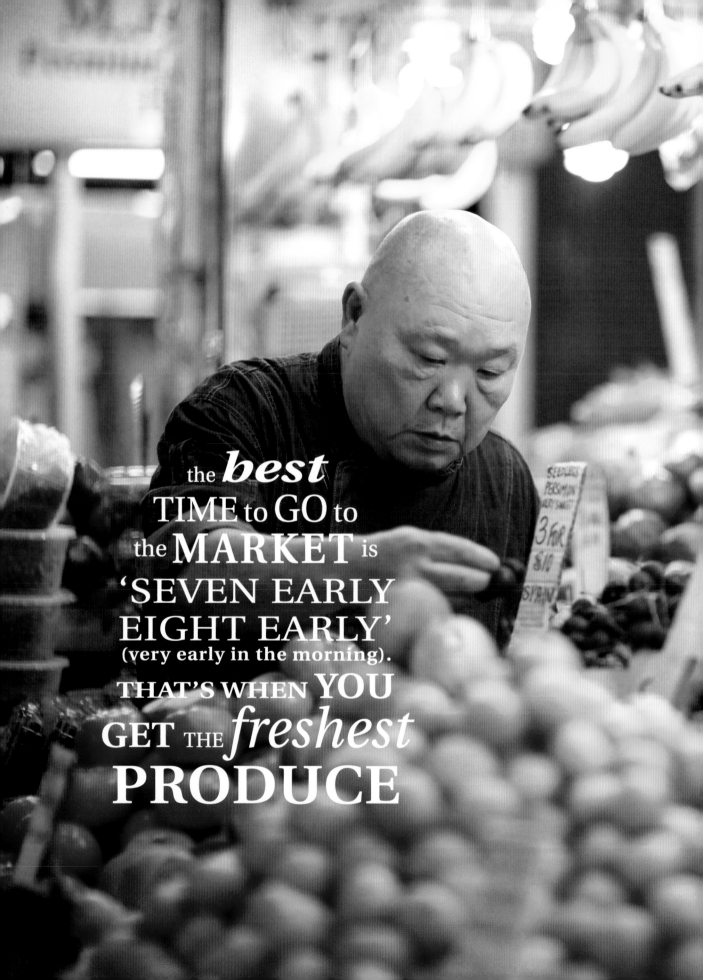

the *best* TIME to GO to the MARKET is 'SEVEN EARLY EIGHT EARLY' (very early in the morning). THAT'S WHEN YOU GET THE *freshest* PRODUCE

For more than a decade, I tried to perfect this recipe, and now, I've finally done it. The key ingredients are laksa leaves, lemongrass and chilli paste (*cili boh*). Packaged chilli paste can be purchased from some wet markets, but take note that there are two types available; get the one without vinegar.

STINGRAY ASAM PEDAS

Serves 4–5

INGREDIENTS

2 Tbsp cooking oil

150 g (5⅓ oz) store-bought chilli paste (*cili boh*)

1 stalk lemongrass, white bulbous section only, halved and bruised

50 g (1¾ oz) tamarind paste, mixed with 400 ml (13⅓ fl oz) water and strained

2 slices dried sour fruit (*asam gelugur*)

A generous handful of laksa leaves (*daun kesom*)

600 g (1 lb 5⅓ oz) stingray fins, cut into 8 pieces

6 slices pineapple

1 medium tomato, cut into wedges

4 ladies' fingers, halved

SPICE PASTE

2.5-cm (1-in) knob ginger, peeled and sliced

3 cloves garlic, peeled and sliced

150 g (5⅓ oz) shallots, peeled and sliced

5 bird's eye chillies

SEASONING

1 Tbsp ground toasted coconut (*kerisek*), see Note on page 70

1 tsp dried anchovy (*ikan bilis*) powder

1 Tbsp sea salt

2 Tbsp sugar

2 Tbsp cooking oil

METHOD

1. Using a food processor, process all ingredients for spice paste into a paste. Heat oil in a pan over medium heat. Add spice paste, chilli paste and lemongrass and stir-fry until fragrant.

2. When paste starts to splatter, add tamarind water, dried sour fruit and laksa leaves. Bring to a boil over high heat. Add ingredients for seasoning and mix well.

3. Lower heat and add stingray. Simmer for 10 minutes or until stingray is cooked. Add pineapple, tomato and ladies' fingers. Simmer for another 5 minutes.

4. Dish out and serve with white rice.

How do you like Singapore's national dish? I like my chilli crab sauce on the sweet and tangy side as it goes very well with Chinese steamed buns (*man tou*). Making a good chilli crab sauce is no rocket science; half the battle is won using my chicken rice chilli sauce (page 56).

CHILLI CRAB

Serves 2–3

INGREDIENTS

750 g (1 lb 11 oz) mud crab, cleaned and cut into 4–6 pieces

Cooking oil, as needed

3 cloves garlic, peeled and chopped

4 Tbsp Hainanese chicken rice chilli sauce (page 56)

2 tsp light soy sauce

1 tsp chicken seasoning powder

1 Tbsp water

150 g (5^1/$_3$ oz) tomato ketchup

1^1/$_2$ Tbsp sugar

1 Tbsp tapioca flour, mixed with 1 Tbsp water

3 eggs, beaten

GARNISH

1 spring onion (scallion), finely sliced

1 red chilli, finely sliced

1 sprig coriander leaves (cilantro), chopped

METHOD

1. Place crabs in a steamer and steam for 6 minutes or until meat does not stick to shell. Turn off heat and let crab sit in steamer with lid on for about 2 minutes.

2. Heat 2 Tbsp oil in a pan over medium heat. Add garlic and stir-fry garlic until fragrant. Add steamed crab and Hainanese chicken rice chilli. Stir to coat crab well.

3. Add light soy sauce, chicken seasoning powder and water. Bring to a boil, then add tomato ketchup and sugar. Add tapioca flour slurry to thicken sauce.

4. Turn off heat and add eggs. Stir well to mix egg into sauce.

5. Dish out and garnish with spring onion, chillies and coriander. Serve as part of a meal with white rice or fried Chinese steamed buns (*man tou*).

TIP Many restaurants tend to fry the crab before simmering it in the sauce, but I prefer to steam it. Steaming typically takes no more than 6 minutes for a regular-sized crab. Not only is steamed crabmeat juicier, the shell also comes off more easily. With frying, the meat tends to stick to the shell.

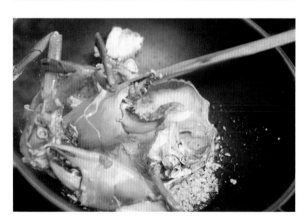

This vegetable dish will not be complete without the spiced coconut (*serunding kelapa*). Making good spiced coconut takes a while, so do this only when you have time to spare. Keep the heat low as the coconut burns easily. Fry it slowly and keep stirring. Your patience will pay off.

SAYUR LODEH

Serves 4–5

INGREDIENTS

2 Tbsp cooking oil

1 litre (32 fl oz / 4 cups) water

150 g (5⅓ oz) long beans, cut into 5-cm (2-in) lengths

150 g (5⅓ oz) yam bean, peeled and cut into cubes

300 g (11 oz) cabbage, cut into large pieces

150 g (5⅓ oz) carrots, peeled and cut into chunks

4 fried tofu puffs, cut into triangles

500 ml (16 fl oz / 2 cups) coconut milk

1 Tbsp salt

2 tsp sugar

2 tsp chicken seasoning powder

2 Tbsp *sambal tumis* (page 74)

SPICED COCONUT

2 cloves garlic, peeled, sliced

2 shallots, peeled, sliced

1 stalk lemongrass, ends trimmed and bruised

2.5-cm (1-in) knob turmeric, peeled

2.5-cm (1-in) knob ginger, peeled

2.5-cm (1-in) knob galangal, peeled

3 Tbsp tamarind water

1 Tbsp cooking oil

1 Tbsp coriander powder

2 kaffir lime leaves

200 g (7 oz) grated coconut

2½ Tbsp sugar

1 tsp salt

1 Tbsp store-bought chilli paste (*cili boh*)

SPICE PASTE

1 lemongrass, ends trimmed and bruised

4 candlenuts

2.5-cm (1-in) knob turmeric, peeled

4-cm (1.5-in) knob ginger, peeled

5 g (⅙ oz) dried prawn paste (*belacan*), toasted

4 cloves garlic, peeled and sliced

8 shallots, peeled and sliced

20 g (⅔ oz) dried prawns (*hae bee*)

100 ml (3½ fl oz) water

METHOD

1. Prepare spiced coconut. Using a food processor, process garlic, shallots, lemongrass, turmeric, ginger and galangal into a paste. Add tamarind water and oil. Mix well. Place mixture in a pan with coriander powder and kaffir lime leaves. Fry over low heat until mixture is dry. Add grated coconut, sugar, salt and chilli paste. Stir continuously until mixture is golden brown. Set aside.

2. Prepare spice paste. Process all ingredients into a paste. Heat oil in a pan over medium heat. Add spice paste and stir-fry until fragrant. Add water and all vegetables except tofu puffs. Add coconut milk, salt, sugar and chicken seasoning powder. Continue to stir until mixture comes to a boil. Stir in *sambal tumis* and add tofu puffs.

3. Dish out and garnish with spiced coconut. Serve with white rice.

The first time I ate this dish was at a Eurasian friend's home.
I still remember how good it tasted with piping hot steamed rice.
I don't prepare this often, but when I do, I enjoy eating it very much.

EURASIAN PRAWN AND PINEAPPLE CURRY

Serves 4–5

INGREDIENTS

2 Tbsp cooking oil

480 g (16 oz) store-bought chilli paste (*cili boh*)

100 g (3½ oz) tamarind paste, mixed with 200 ml (6⅔ fl oz) water and strained

1 small pineapple, peeled and cut into cubes

1½ Tbsp English mustard

2½ Tbsp sugar

1 Tbsp salt

2 tsp chicken seasoning powder

18 large sea prawns, peeled and deveined, leaving tails intact

SPICE PASTE

4 medium red onions, peeled and sliced

4 candlenuts

4 cloves garlic, peeled and sliced

2-cm (¾-in) knob galangal, peeled

2.5-cm (1-in) knob ginger, peeled

2.5-cm (1-in) knob turmeric, peeled

5 g (⅙ oz) dried prawn paste (*belacan*), toasted

2 stalks lemongrass, ends trimmed and bruised

100 ml (3½ fl oz) water

METHOD

1. Using a food processor, process all ingredients for spice paste into a paste. Heat oil in a wok over medium heat. Add spice paste and chilli paste and stir-fry until fragrant.

2. Add tamarind water, pineapple cubes, mustard, sugar and salt. Mix well and bring to a simmer over low heat. Add chicken seasoning powder and mix well.

3. Add sea prawns and continue to cook for another 5 minutes or until prawns are cooked through.

4. Dish out and serve with white rice.

I've traded tips with many chefs on making *mee siam*, and the most surprising trick I learnt was to add sweet chilli sauce. I also add a handful of dried anchovies (*ikan bilis*) and dried prawns (*hae bee*) to make the gravy really tasty. *Sedap!*

MEE SIAM

Serves 6–8

INGREDIENTS

400 g (14⅓ oz) dried rice vermicelli (*bee hoon*)

250 g (9 oz) bean sprouts

2–3 drops red food colouring

3–4 hard-boiled eggs, peeled and halved

3 fried tofu puffs, cut into small cubes

Chinese chives, chopped

5 calamansi limes, halved

GRAVY

10 g (⅓ oz) dried anchovies (*ikan bilis*)

10 g (⅓ oz) dried prawns (*hae bee*)

30 g (1 oz) roasted peanuts, skinned

250 g (9 oz) shallots, peeled and sliced

7 cloves garlic, peeled and sliced

Cooking oil, as needed

300 g (11 oz) *sambal tumis* (page 74)

300 g (11 oz) tamarind paste, mixed with 1.8 litres (60 fl oz) water and strained

8 pieces dried sour fruit (*asam gelugur*)

4 Tbsp fermented soy bean paste

1 stalk lemongrass, ends trimmed and bruised

400 g (14⅓ oz) sugar

3 Tbsp sweet chilli sauce

METHOD

1. Prepare gravy. Using a food processor, process dried anchovies, dried prawns and roasted peanuts until fine. Set mixture aside and process shallots and garlic into a paste with a little oil.

2. Heat 2 Tbsp oil in a pan over medium heat and stir-fry *sambal tumis* until fragrant. Add ground anchovy and ground shallot mixtures and stir-fry until fragrant. Add tamarind water and remaining gravy ingredients and bring to a boil. Lower heat and simmer for 30 minutes.

3. Soak rice vermicelli in water until softened. Drain and blanch in boiling water for 5 minutes. Drain and cool vermicelli under running water. Drain and place in a large pot. Add red food colouring and mix well. Set aside.

4. Blanch bean sprouts in boiling water for about 2 minutes. Drain.

5. To serve, place some vermicelli in a serving bowl. Top with gravy and garnish with hard-boiled egg, cubes of fried tofu puffs and chopped Chinese chives. Finish with a drizzle of lime juice.

As a kid, I often had *mee rebus* for breakfast. Back then, a bowl of these noodles cost only 10 to 15 cents! It is my comfort food. Sadly, Tanglin Halt market, where my favourite *mee rebus* stall is located, will soon be demolished. The lady who runs the stall is Cik Maria and this recipe was created with the many tips she shared with me.

MEE REBUS

Serves 4–5

INGREDIENTS

1½ Tbsp meat curry powder

200 g (7 oz) fermented soy bean paste

2 Tbsp *sambal tumis* (page 74)

1.4 litres (46 fl oz) water

1 Tbsp dark soy sauce

4 Tbsp sugar

2 Tbsp cornflour mixed with 200 ml (6⅔ fl oz) water

1 kg (2 lb 3 oz) yellow egg noodles

100 g (3½ oz) bean sprouts

2 squares firm bean curd, pan-fried and cut into small cubes

2–3 Tbsp fried shallots

1 stalk Chinese celery

2–3 green chillies, sliced

4–5 hard-boiled eggs, peeled and halved

4–5 calamansi limes, halved

MEE REBUS GRAVY

7 shallots, peeled and sliced

4 cloves garlic, peeled and sliced

20 candlenuts

2.5-cm (1-in) knob turmeric, peeled

10 g (⅓ oz) dried prawns (*hae bee*)

10 g (⅓ oz) tiny dried shrimp (*grago*)

5 g (⅙ oz) dried anchovies (*ikan bilis*)

5 g (⅙ oz) dried prawn paste (*belacan*), toasted

TIP Tasty *mee rebus* gravy has a good balance of dried anchovies (*ikan bilis*), tiny dried shrimp (*grago*) and dried prawns (*hae bee*); so don't miss these ingredients out.

METHOD

1. Prepare *mee rebus* gravy. Using a food processor, process all ingredients for *mee rebus* gravy into a paste. Add meat curry powder and fermented soy bean paste and mix well.

2. Transfer paste to a pot. Add *sambal tumis* and stir gently over low heat. Add water, dark soy sauce and sugar. Bring to a boil, then stir in corn flour slurry to thicken gravy. Simmer for about 30 minutes.

3. Blanch noodles and bean sprouts and divide among serving bowls. Ladle hot gravy over.

4. Top with firm bean curd, fried shallots, green chillies, hard-boiled eggs and calamansi halves. Serve.

Fenugreek leaves are hard to come by and sometimes it takes me more than half a day to find a store that stocks it. Still, I refuse to replace it with other herbs because it has a unique flavour. Fenugreek doesn't smell that great on its own, but it completes butter chicken.

INDIAN BUTTER CHICKEN

Serves 4–5

INGREDIENTS

4 cloves garlic, peeled and sliced

2.5-cm (1-in) knob ginger, peeled

1 Tbsp sea salt

2 Tbsp chilli powder

5 chicken drumsticks, cut into pieces

1 Tbsp cooking oil

10 g (⅓ oz) butter

Dried fenugreek leaves, as needed

Cooking cream, as needed

GRAVY

1 red onion, peeled and sliced

5 tomatoes, peeled

2 Tbsp dried fenugreek leaves

750 ml (24 fl oz / 3 cups) water

1 Tbsp garam masala

20 g (⅔ oz) cashew nuts

1 Tbsp sea salt

2 tsp sugar

125 g (4½ oz) butter

250 ml (8 fl oz / 1 cup) cooking cream

1 Tbsp plain yoghurt

METHOD

1. Using a food processor, process garlic and ginger into a paste. Mix half the garlic-ginger paste with salt and chilli powder and rub mixture over chicken. Set aside to marinade for 10 minutes.

2. Heat oil in a large pan over medium heat. Add butter and when butter becomes foamy, add chicken and cook slowly until chicken caramelizes to a dark brown. Remove chicken and set aside.

3. Prepare gravy. Using the same pan, add remaining garlic-ginger paste and red onion. Stir-fry until fragrant. Add peeled tomatoes, dried fenugreek leaves and water. Add garam masala, cashew nuts and salt. Cook until tomatoes soften. Add sugar, butter and cooking cream. Cook for another 2–3 minutes.

4. Transfer gravy to a mixing bowl. Using an immersion blender, blend gravy until it starts to become foamy. Pass gravy through a sieve to remove any lumps. Pour gravy into a pan and bring to a simmer over medium-low heat.

5. Add chicken and yoghurt to simmering gravy. Cover and continue to simmer for about 15 minutes or until chicken is cooked through.

6. Dish out and sprinkle with dried fenugreek leaves and a drizzle of cooking cream. Serve with basmati rice or naan.

Although there are many steps to making this dish, it is really not difficult.
I am generous with my use of saffron, which makes the rice very fragrant.
I'm proud to say my Malay and Indian-Muslim friends love my dum biryani.

DUM BIRYANI

Serves 6–8

INGREDIENTS

8 chicken drumsticks

Water, as needed

4 Tbsp salt

1 kg (2 lb 3 oz) basmati rice, rinsed

A pinch of saffron, soaked in 150 ml (5 fl oz) hot water

A handful of cashew nuts, fried shallots, golden raisins and chopped coriander leaves (cilantro)

CHICKEN MARINADE

7.5-cm (3-in) knob ginger, peeled and sliced

6 cloves garlic, peeled and chopped

40 g (1½ oz) fried shallots

3 Tbsp garam masala

3 Tbsp chilli powder

2 medium tomatoes, chopped

1 sprig coriander leaves (cilantro), finely chopped

1 cinnamon stick

10 cardamom pods

½ Tbsp caraway seeds

15 Tbsp plain yoghurt

4 green chillies

15 cloves

1 bay leaf

1 Tbsp sugar

1 Tbsp cooking oil

METHOD

1. Prepare chicken marinade. Using a food processor, process ginger, garlic and fried shallots into a paste. Mix with remaining ingredients and rub all over chicken. Cover and set chicken aside for 1 hour.

2. Place chicken in a large pot. Add sufficient water to cover chicken, then cook over low heat for about 5 minutes. Chicken should still be slightly pink. Skim at least 6 Tbsp excess chilli oil from surface of liquid and set aside.

3. Half-fill a clean pan with water. Add salt and rice and cook over medium heat for about 6 minutes.

4. Spoon one-third of rice over chicken in pot. Press down evenly. Repeat to add another one-third of rice, then layer with remaining rice. Pour saffron water and skimmed chilli oil over rice. Lower heat and cook for 20 minutes.

5. When rice is done, turn off heat and let rest for 15 minutes before serving. Garnish with cashew nuts, fried shallots, golden raisins and finely chopped coriander leaves.

TIP The method of making dum biryani is actually similar to preparing Chinese clay pot rice. During the steaming process, make sure the heat is properly distributed by shifting the pot regularly.

ZI CHAR & ASIAN CLASSICS

Over the years,
I've learnt to cook many things.
But I am, at heart, a *zi char* chef.

This dish was a hot favourite at Goshen, my first restaurant. Till today, old customers still tell me that they miss it. Freshwater fish, like song fish, tend to have an earthy taste that some do not fancy. To remove traces of this taste, drain away the excess liquid from the fish head after steaming.

STEAMED SONG FISH HEAD

Serves 4–5

INGREDIENTS

1 medium song fish head, cleaned
1 Tbsp cooking oil
3 cloves garlic, peeled and sliced
2.5-cm (1-in) knob ginger, peeled and finely chopped
1 Tbsp tapioca flour, mixed with 1 Tbsp water
1 Tbsp fried pork lard

SAUCE

3 salted plums
3 Tbsp fermented bean paste
1 Tbsp tangerine sauce
5 Tbsp sugar
2 Tbsp calamansi juice
2 bird's eye chillies, chopped
$\frac{1}{2}$ tsp dark soy sauce
125 ml (4 fl oz / $\frac{1}{2}$ cup) water

GARNISH

1 spring onion (scallion), cut into thin strips
1 red chilli, cut into thin strips
1 sprig coriander leaves (cilantro), chopped

METHOD

1. Place fish head on a shallow steaming plate and steam for 14 minutes over high heat. Remove fish from steamer and carefully drain away steaming liquid.

2. Heat oil in a pan over medium heat. Add garlic and ginger and stir-fry until fragrant. Add ingredients for sauce and simmer until fragrant. Add tapioca flour slurry and stir to thicken sauce.

3. Pour sauce over steamed fish head. Top with fried pork lard and garnish with spring onion, red chillies and coriander. Serve as part of a meal.

Don't let the shells intimidate you — crayfish are actually very easy to cook!
The fishmonger will help you chop and clean the crayfish if you ask.
Remember to add curry leaves, because they make the dish extra fragrant.

BLACK PEPPER CRAYFISH

Serves 2–3

INGREDIENTS

2 large crayfish

Sea salt as needed

Ground black pepper as
needed

125 ml (4 fl oz / ½ cup)
cooking oil

2 Tbsp butter

2 cloves garlic, peeled and
chopped

1 tsp chicken seasoning
powder

1 Tbsp tapioca flour, mixed
with 1 Tbsp water

BLACK PEPPER SAUCE

2 Tbsp ground black pepper

1 Tbsp oyster sauce

2 tsp abalone bouillon

1 Tbsp dark soy sauce

1 Tbsp light soy sauce

1 Tbsp sugar

5 Tbsp water

GARNISH

A few lettuce leaves

1 red chilli, cut into thin
strips

METHOD

1. Scrub crayfish well to clean, then cut lengthwise
in half. Rub with some salt and black pepper.

2. Heat oil in a pan over high heat. Add crayfish and deep-
fry until crayfish is golden brown. Drain and set aside.

3. Leave 2 Tbsp oil in pan and reheat over medium heat.
Add butter and when it begins to sizzle, add garlic and
stir-fry for a few moments until golden brown.

4. Add ingredients for black pepper sauce to pan and
mix well. Bring to the boil, then add crayfish and stir-fry
over high heat until crayfish is well coated with sauce.

5. Add chicken seasoning powder, followed by tapioca
flour slurry to thicken sauce. Continue to stir-fry until
sauce is reduced.

6. Dish out and garnish with lettuce and chillies.
Serve as part of a meal.

IN COOKING, there are INGREDIENTS YOU can SUBSTITUTE and then there are SOME INGREDIENTS that *SIMPLY CANNOT* BE REPLACED. It is OKAY TO IMPROVISE, but *DON'T MESS* with the CLASSICS!

I honestly think that commercial bouillon and stocks are the best inventions of the 21st century. I don't shy away from using ready-made bouillon and stocks from the supermarkets because it saves a lot of time. This recipe is very simple. Crabmeat is naturally sweet, so you'll need just a little bit of sauce made using abalone bouillon to bring out the flavour.

CLAY POT CRAB WITH GLASS NOODLES

Serves 3–4

INGREDIENTS

150 g (5⅓ oz) glass noodles
Cooking oil, as needed
4 cloves garlic, peeled and chopped
3 shallots, peeled and sliced
3 slices ginger
200 ml (6⅔ fl oz) water
1 Sri Lankan mud crab, about 800 g (1¾ lb), cleaned and cut into 4–6 pieces
1 tsp abalone bouillon
1 tsp oyster sauce
2 tsp dark soy sauce
1 tsp light soy sauce
1 tsp chicken seasoning powder
Pork lard, as desired

GARNISH

1 spring onion (scallion), cut into thin strips
1 sprig coriander leaves (cilantro), chopped

METHOD

1. Soak glass noodles in water for 20 minutes until softened, Drain and set aside.

2. Heat oil in a clay pot over medium heat. Add garlic, shallots and ginger and stir-fry until fragrant. Add water and bring to a boil.

3. When water is boiling, add crab, abalone bouillon, oyster sauce, dark soy sauce, light soy sauce and chicken seasoning powder. Lower heat and simmer for 5 minutes.

4. Add glass noodles and stir well to mix. Cover pot with a lid and simmer for another 5 minutes until glass noodles soak up stock. Add a little pork lard for flavour if desired.

5. Garnish with spring onion and coriander leaves. Serve immediately.

This is my favourite Chinese New Year dish that my family and I enjoyed eating when I was young. Abalone was cheap then, but prices have escalated over the years. In a way, this is a lesson in life – to not take things that we have for granted.

BRAISED ABALONE, HONG KONG-STYLE

Serves 3–4

INGREDIENTS

1 tsp sugar

1 medium carrot, peeled and sliced

3 baby corn cobs

25 g (⁴/₅ oz) snow peas

2 Tbsp cooking oil

1 clove garlic, peeled and chopped

1 medium red onion, peeled and cut into quarters

1 can (425 g / 14 oz) braised abalone

1 tsp tapioca flour mixed with 1 tsp water

A drizzle of Shaoxing wine

SAUCE

2 tsp light soy sauce

1 tsp oyster sauce

1 tsp abalone bouillon

4 Tbsp abalone broth from canned abalone

1 tsp sugar

METHOD

1. Boil a pot of water and add sugar. Blanch carrot, baby corn and snow peas in boiling water. Drain vegetables and place under running water to cool and stop the cooking process.

2. Heat oil in a pan over medium heat. Add garlic, onion and blanched carrot, baby corn and snow peas. Stir-fry until fragrant.

3. Combine all ingredients for sauce in a bowl.

4. Add abalone to pan. Add sauce and mix well. Add tapioca flour slurry to thicken sauce. Let simmer for 2 minutes.

5. Finish with a drizzle of Shaoxing wine. Dish out and serve as part of a meal.

TIP For perfectly blanched vegetables, plunge them into boiling water for a couple of minutes, then immediately transfer to a bowl of iced water. Adding sugar to the boiling water also helps prevent discolouration.

Restaurant-grade dishes, like this one, can also be
prepared at home. Make sure you get fresh lobster and
keep the shells for plating. Your guests will be impressed.
The noodles are the same kind used in *wanton mee*, and can
be found at most Chinese provision shops that sell dry goods.

LOBSTER SHANG MEEN

Serves 2

INGREDIENTS

200 g (7 oz) Hong Kong noodles
Cooking oil, as needed
2 cloves garlic, peeled and chopped
1 litre (32 fl oz / 4 cups) water
400 g (14$\frac{1}{3}$ oz) lobster, cut into pieces
3 baby Shanghai greens
1 tsp fish bouillon
2 tsp sea salt
1 egg, beaten
1$\frac{1}{2}$ Tbsp cornflour, mixed with 3 Tbsp water
A drizzle of Shaoxing wine
A dash of ground white pepper

METHOD

1. Boil noodles until al dente. Drain well. Heat sufficient oil for
deep-frying in a deep pan or wok over medium heat. Gently lower
noodles into hot oil and deep-fry until light brown and crispy.
Drain well and place on a large serving plate. Set aside.

2. Leave 1 Tbsp oil in the pan or wok and reheat over medium
heat. Add garlic and stir-fry until fragrant. Add water and bring
to a boil. Add lobster and baby Shanghai greens. The water should
cover the lobster. Add more water if needed.

3. Simmer until lobster changes colour and is cooked. Add fish
bouillon and salt. Mix well. Add cornflour slurry and simmer
to thicken sauce. Stir in egg.

4. Place lobster on top of crispy Hong Kong noodles. Ladle sauce
over, then finish with a drizzle of Shaoxing wine and a dash of
white pepper. Serve immediately.

My version of this dish does not include Sichuan pepper and the main star is dried chilli. Don't worry that the oil turns black as you fry the chilli. It's supposed to happen. I recommend using Jamie Oliver's balsamic vinegar – its sweetness works very well in this dish.

KUNG PO CHICKEN

Serves 4–5

INGREDIENTS

600 g (1 lb 5⅓ oz) skinless, boneless chicken fillet, cut into chunks

10 dried chillies, cut in half, seeds discarded

Cooking oil, as needed

3 cloves garlic, peeled and chopped

1 medium red onion, peeled and sliced

½ red capsicum (bell pepper), cored and diced

½ green capsicum (bell pepper), cored and diced

3 spring onions (scallions), white part only, cut into short lengths

150 g (5⅓ oz) roasted cashew nuts

5 Tbsp balsamic vinegar

1 Tbsp sugar

1 Tbsp oyster sauce

A drizzle of Shaoxing wine

MARINADE

½ Tbsp ground white pepper

2½ Tbsp light soy sauce

1 tsp sugar

2 tsp sesame oil

1 Tbsp Shaoxing wine

1 Tbsp tapioca flour, mixed with 1 Tbsp water

METHOD

1. Combine ingredients for marinade in a bowl. Add chicken and mix well. Cover and refrigerate for 30 minutes.

2. Boil a pot of water and boil dried chillies to soften. Drain well and set aside.

3. Heat sufficient oil for deep-frying in a pan over medium heat. Add marinated chicken and deep-fry until golden and crisp. Drain well and set aside.

4. Reheat oil over medium heat. Add dried chillies and stir-fry until dried chillies and oil are black. Drain oil, leaving 2 Tbsp oil in pan.

5. Reheat oil over medium heat. Add garlic and chicken and stir-fry lightly. Add red onion, capsicums, spring onions and cashew nuts. Stir-fry to mix, then add balsamic vinegar, sugar and oyster sauce. Lower heat and simmer until sauce thickens. Add a drizzle of Shaoxing wine. Mix well.

6. Dish out and serve as part of a meal with white rice.

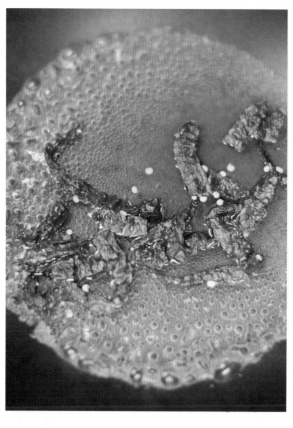

Whenever I visit Hong Kong, I must eat this dish. After chatting with many Cantonese chefs, I have discovered how they maintain the quality of the stew. The traditional formula is handed down quite literally, from pot to pot. A portion of the previous stew is always retained and added to the new batch to ensure that the sauce continues to taste like the original. As for my version, the secret ingredient is peanut butter!

STEWED BEEF BRISKET

Serves 4–5

INGREDIENTS

1 kg (2 lb 3 oz) beef brisket
1 Tbsp cooking oil
5 cloves garlic, peeled and chopped
4 thick slices ginger, peeled
3 star anise
3 cinnamon sticks
10 white peppercorns
1 cube red fermented bean curd
2 pieces tangerine peel, soaked and cut into strips
1 litre (32 fl oz / 4 cups) water
500 g (1 lb 1½ oz) radish, peeled and cut into triangular wedges

SEASONING

½ Tbsp *chu hou* paste
1 Tbsp oyster sauce
½ Tbsp dark soy sauce
1 Tbsp light soy sauce
½ Tbsp sugar
1 Tbsp peanut butter

METHOD

1. Blanch beef brisket in a large pot of boiling water for about 8 minutes to remove any impurities. Drain and set aside.

2. Heat oil in a saucepan over medium heat. Add garlic and ginger and stir-fry until fragrant. Add star anise, cinnamon, white peppercorns, red fermented bean curd and tangerine peel. Add blanched beef brisket and water.

3. Add ingredients for seasoning and mix well. Cover with a lid, turn to low heat and simmer for 2½ hours.

4. Add radish and top up with enough water to cover meat and radish. Replace cover and continue to simmer for another 1 hour until radish is tender.

5. Dish out and garnish as desired. Serve as part of a meal.

NOTE *Chu hou* paste is a popular condiment used in Cantonese cooking. It is made from fermented soy beans, white fermented bean curd, garlic, ginger and spices and adds that extra depth of flavour to stewed dishes like this one. *Chu hou* paste is available in the paste and marinade section of some supermarkets.

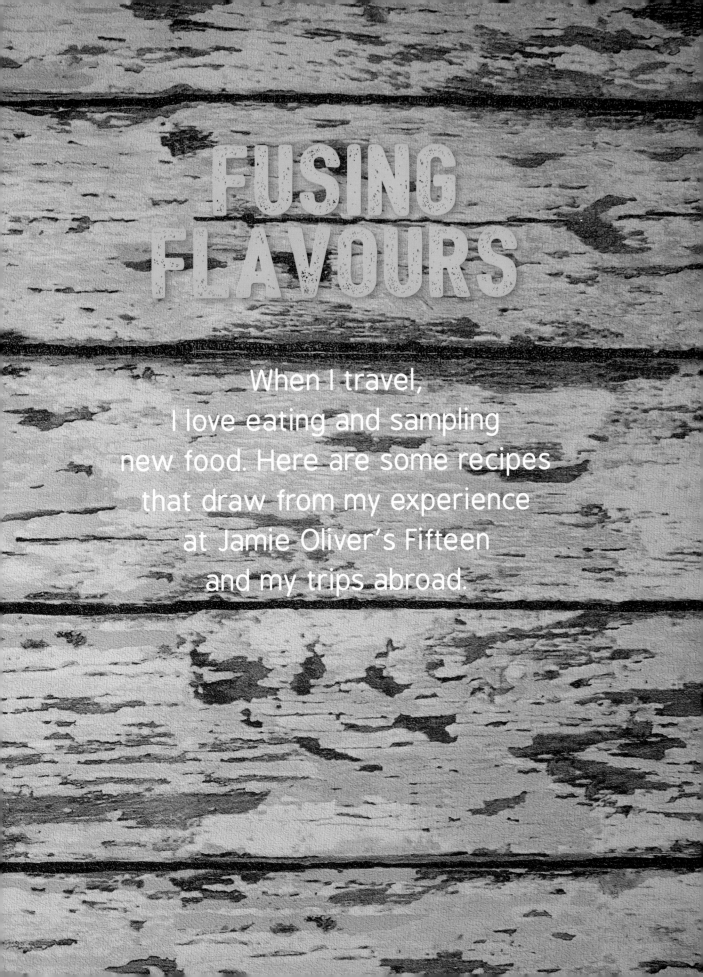

FUSING FLAVOURS

When I travel,
I love eating and sampling
new food. Here are some recipes
that draw from my experience
at Jamie Oliver's Fifteen
and my trips abroad.

DURING my stint at **JAMIE OLIVER'S FIFTEEN,** we visited an abattoir in Wales to learn about **MEAT CUTS & MEAT AGEING.** It was **A REAL EYE OPENER**

Before my stint at Fifteen, I didn't know much about Western cuisine. I generally prefer Asian food, but braised oxtail is definitely one of my few favourite Western dishes. Perhaps it's because I love meat with bones in it. This is really tasty – try it for yourself!

BRAISED OXTAIL

Serves 4–5

INGREDIENTS

1 oxtail, about 750 g
  (1 lb 11 oz), cut into 5 pieces
Sea salt, as needed
Ground black pepper, as needed
2 Tbsp cooking oil
4 cloves garlic, peeled and
  chopped
1 celery stick, chopped
1 medium red onion, peeled
  and quartered
1 medium swede
  (Swedish turnip), peeled
  and cut into chunks

1 sprig rosemary
1 sprig thyme
400 ml (13¹⁄₃ fl oz) dry
  red wine
300 ml (10 fl oz / 1¹⁄₄ cups)
  beef stock
100 g (3¹⁄₂ oz) streaky bacon,
  cut into small pieces
5 button mushrooms, halved
6 heirloom carrots
1 sprig coriander leaves
  (cilantro), chopped

METHOD

1. Preheat oven to 200°C (400°F).

2. Rub oxtail with a little salt and black pepper. Heat 1 Tbsp oil in a pan and add oxtail. Sear until oxtail is browned.

3. Remove oxtail from pan and place in an ovenproof casserole. Add 2 cloves garlic, celery, onion, swede, rosemary, thyme, red wine and beef stock. Season with salt and black pepper. Cover casserole and place in oven. Lower oven temperature to 175°C (350°F) and braise for about 1 hour.

4. After casserole has been in the oven for about an hour, heat 1 Tbsp oil in a clean pan over medium heat. Add bacon, remaining 2 cloves garlic and button mushrooms and sauté until golden brown. Add to casserole together with carrots and continue to braise for another 2 hours until oxtail is fork-tender.

5. Garnish with coriander and serve.

I was gunning for shock appeal when I came up with this dish. Tasty fried rice has a lovely char smell (*wok hei*), and you can create that distinctive flavour by following my recipe. The first thing I learnt to cook as a child was fried rice, so you can take my word for it.

HEART ATTACK FRIED RICE
WITH WAGYU BEEF

Serves 2

INGREDIENTS

1 tsp olive oil

50 g (1¾ oz) butter

1 clove garlic, peeled and
chopped

200 g (7 oz) cooked white rice,
chilled

½ tsp chicken seasoning
powder

1 tsp dark soy sauce

Fresh salad

1 spring onion (scallion),
finely chopped

WAGYU BEEF

300 g (11 oz) Wagyu striploin
steak

A pinch of sea salt

A dash of ground black pepper

1 Tbsp olive oil

10 g (⅓ oz) butter

1 sprig thyme

METHOD

1. Heat olive oil in a wok over medium heat. Add butter
and when butter is melted and foamy, add garlic and
sauté until fragrant.

2. Add cooked white rice and stir-fry to heat through and
break up any lumps. Add chicken seasoning powder and
dark soy sauce. Continue to stir-fry until rice is evenly
coated with dark soy sauce. Dish out and set aside.

3. Prepare beef. Season beef with salt, black pepper and a
drizzle of olive oil.

4. Heat 1 Tbsp olive oil in a frying pan over high heat. Add
beef and cook for 4 minutes on each side or until browned.
Lower to medium-low heat, then add butter and thyme.
Cook for another 1.5 minutes, then remove beef from pan.

5. Cut beef diagonally across grain into thin slices. Serve
with fried rice and a fresh salad. Garnish with spring onion.

TIP Achieving the char smell (*wok hei*) in cooking is
not magic. You just need to get the wok hot enough
to produce smoke that gets transferred to your food.
Invest in a heavy cast iron wok or pan.

WHEN
I WAS a kid,
I USED TO THINK
LAMB
CHOPS &
KARATE
CHOPS were
the *SAME*
THING

My wife is not a fan of lamb, but she savoured every bit of this dish when I made it. Choose a lamb rack with a cap of fat on one side; it will cook better than a Frenched rack (also described as "cap off"). Remember to let the meat rest after removing from the oven so that it will be juicier and tastier when you cut it.

BABY LAMB RACK WITH COUSCOUS

Serves 3–4

INGREDIENTS

500 g (1 lb ½ oz) New Zealand baby lamb rack
A pinch of sea salt
A dash of ground black pepper
Olive oil, as needed
4 heirloom carrots

MINT GREMOLATA

A handful of mint leaves, chopped
1 tsp finely chopped capers
1 Tbsp grated lemon zest
Juice from ½ lemon
2 cloves garlic, peeled and finely chopped

3 Tbsp extra virgin olive oil
Sea salt, to taste
Ground black pepper, to taste

COUSCOUS

100 g (3½ oz) instant couscous
125 ml (4 fl oz / ½ cup) lamb jus, made using 1 tsp lamb bouillon mixed with 125 ml (4 fl oz / ½ cup) water
A pinch of sea salt
A dash of ground black pepper
1 Tbsp olive oil
Boiling water, as needed
1 Tbsp black raisins

METHOD

1. Preheat oven to 180°C (350°F). Season lamb with salt, black pepper and a drizzle of olive oil. Heat 4 Tbsp oil in a cast iron grill pan over medium heat. Place lamb skin-side down in pan and sear for 2–3 minutes on each side. Remove from heat. Add carrots and place pan in the oven to bake for 18 minutes.

2. Prepare mint gremolata. Mix all ingredients for mint gremolata in a bowl. Set aside for flavours to develop.

3. Prepare couscous. Place couscous in a bowl. Add lamb jus, salt, black pepper, olive oil and enough boiling water to make up amount of liquid specified on instructions on packet. Mix well and cover bowl tightly. Set aside for 25 minutes. Fluff with a fork.

4. Serve lamb with couscous, carrots and mint gremolata.

Indonesian dark soy sauce or *kicap manis* is a staple condiment that goes very well with grilled dishes. In this recipe, I've used the sweet dark sauce as a glaze for the salmon, and it balances the flavour of the fish perfectly.

PAN-FRIED SALMON WITH DARK SOY SAUCE AND STARFRUIT SALSA

Serves 1

INGREDIENTS

200 g (7 oz) salmon
Sea salt, as needed
Ground black pepper, as needed
5 Tbsp cooking oil
2–3 tsp Indonesian dark soy sauce (*kicap manis*)

STARFRUIT SALSA

1/3 medium cucumber, diced
1 medium red onion, peeled and diced
1 medium star fruit, cut into 15 thin slices
3 Tbsp *sambal belacan* (recipe below)

SAMBAL BELACAN

5 red bird's eye chillies
2–3 shallots, peeled
2–3 cloves garlic, peeled
4 g (1/8 oz) dried prawn paste (*belacan*), toasted
2–3 small green limes, juice extracted
1 red chilli, sliced
1 tsp sugar
1 tsp sweet chilli sauce
1 tsp grated green lime zest

METHOD

1. Prepare *sambal belacan*. Using a food processor, process ingredients for *sambal belacan* into a paste. Set aside for making starfruit salsa.

2. Rinse salmon and pat dry. Score skin to prevent fish from curling while cooking. Season with a pinch of salt and black pepper.

3. Heat oil in a pan over medium-high heat. Gently place salmon skin-side down in pan. Let cook for 2–3 minutes before turning salmon over. Add Indonesian dark soy sauce and let cook for another 2–3 minutes.

4. Prepare starfruit salsa. Toss ingredients together and mix well.

5. Spoon salsa onto a serving plate and arrange salmon on top. Serve.

Braised fennel was often cooked at Fifteen, but it is still relatively uncommon in Singapore. Fennel doesn't have a strong taste on its own, so braising it in the same pan used to sear the sea bass will infuse it with the flavour of the fish. This is a simple and delicious dish that reminds me of Jamie Oliver's cooking style.

PAN-FRIED SEA BASS FILLET with BRAISED FENNEL

Serves 2

INGREDIENTS

300 g (11 oz) sea bass fillet, skin lightly scored
A pinch of sea salt
A dash of ground black pepper
A drizzle of olive oil
2 Tbsp cooking oil
Fennel leaves, to taste

BRAISED FENNEL

1 Tbsp olive oil
1 fennel bulb, halved, then cut each half into 3 pieces
A pinch of sea salt
A dash of ground black pepper

2 tomatoes
3 cloves garlic, peeled and chopped
½ medium red onion, peeled and diced
2 sprigs thyme
4 tsp white wine
1 tsp capers
A slice of lemon
250 ml (8 fl oz / 1 cup) seafood stock
A dollop of butter

METHOD

1. Prepare braised fennel. Heat olive oil in a frying pan over medium heat. Add fennel and season with salt and black pepper. Add tomatoes, garlic, onion, thyme, white wine, capers, lemon and seafood stock. Cover pan with a lid and braise for 20 minutes or until fennel is soft. Add butter and stir to thicken sauce. Dish out to a serving plate and set aside.

2. Season sea bass with salt, black pepper and a drizzle of olive oil. Heat oil in a frying pan over medium heat. Once pan is hot, place sea bass skin-side down and cook until edges of fish turn golden brown. Turn fish over to cook to on the other side.

3. Arrange fish on braised fennel. Garnish with fennel leaves and serve immediately.

ABOUT CHEF BENNY SE TEO

Chef Benny is well known in the Singapore food scene as a chef, restaurateur and social entrepreneur. Featured in local and international media such as the *Straits Times*, BBC and CNN, Benny has also spoken at universities and conferences, including the globally renowned TEDx Talks.

Benny's story is an inspiring tale of humanity, hope and redemption. A high-school dropout, former drug user and ex-convict, Benny has known failure and condemnation. For years, drug addiction controlled Benny's life, but his mother's love remained a constant through those dark days. The turning point came in 1992, when Benny's brush with duodenum cancer delivered a wakeup call, and led him to find absolution in Christianity.

This cookbook is a celebration of the love and fellowship that Benny has experienced in his journey of self-discovery. Growing up, Benny had always been curious about cooking. He knew he had a knack for recreating dishes, but it was not until he served as a tea boy to the prison superintendent that he discovered his creative gift.

With the encouragement of friends and strangers, Benny eventually came to embrace his culinary talent. In 2005, he took a leap of faith to start his first restaurant, Goshen. The following year, Benny secured a place in the apprenticeship programme at Jamie Oliver's Fifteen, a non-profit restaurant in London. Goshen folded shortly after his return to Singapore, but Benny remained undeterred, and went on to co-found Eighteen Chefs—a successful restaurant chain and social enterprise that helps ex-offenders and youths at risk.

Ten years on, Benny now shares his story through this collection of well-loved recipes. Inspired by his Sei Yap (a Cantonese dialect group) and Singaporean heritage, his childhood and many cherished memories, the dishes are packed with nostalgia and punchy flavours. Alongside the recipes, Benny candidly shares practical tips that home cooks will find most handy.

When Benny is not busy cooking up new projects or travelling with his wife, Mei, he can be found chatting with friends over a hot cup of bullet *kopi* (black coffee with butter). Do say hello when you see him. Chef Benny may not be smiling, but don't worry, that's simply his default expression. Remember to tell him how much you enjoyed *Honest Good Food*.

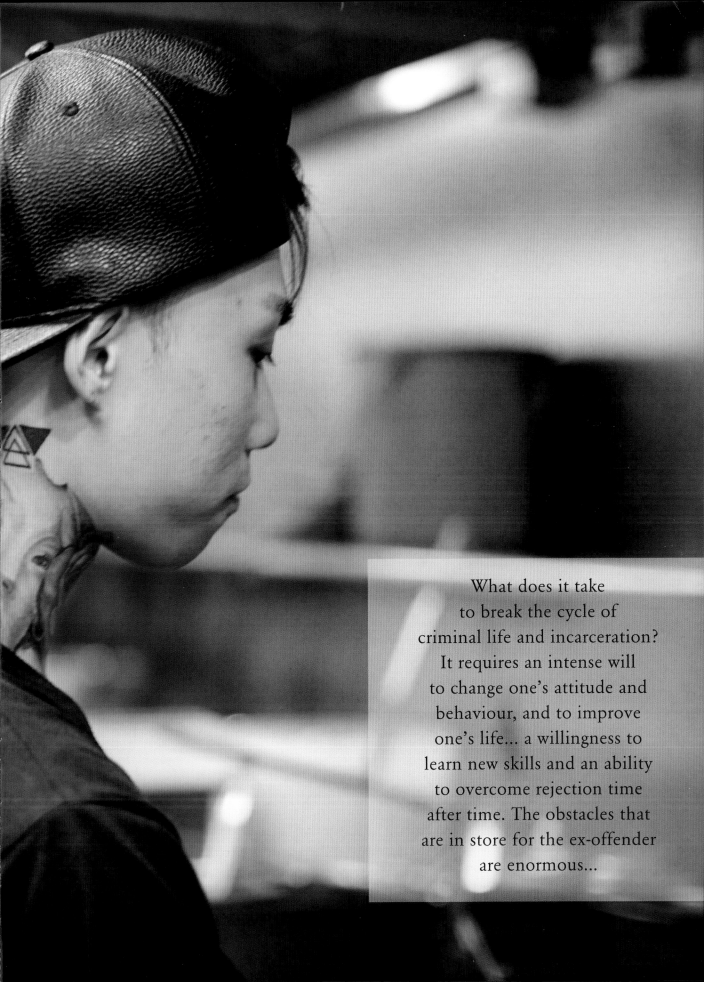

What does it take
to break the cycle of
criminal life and incarceration?
It requires an intense will
to change one's attitude and
behaviour, and to improve
one's life... a willingness to
learn new skills and an ability
to overcome rejection time
after time. The obstacles that
are in store for the ex-offender
are enormous...

WEIGHTS & MEASURES

Quantities for this book are given in Metric and American (spoon and cup) measures. Standard spoon and cup measurements used are: 1 tsp = 5 ml, 1 Tbsp = 15 ml and 1 cup = 250 ml. All measures are level unless otherwise stated.

LIQUID AND VOLUME MEASURES

Metric	Imperial	American
5 ml	$1/6$ fl oz	1 tsp
10 ml	$1/3$ fl oz	1 dessertspoon
15 ml	$1/2$ fl oz	1 Tbsp
60 ml	2 fl oz	$1/4$ cup (4 Tbsp)
85 ml	$2^1/2$ fl oz	$1/3$ cup
90 ml	3 fl oz	$3/8$ cup (6 Tbsp)
125 ml	4 fl oz	$1/2$ cup
180 ml	6 fl oz	$3/4$ cup
250 ml	8 fl oz	1 cup
300 ml	10 fl oz ($1/2$ pint)	$1^1/4$ cups
375 ml	12 fl oz	$1^1/2$ cups
435 ml	14 fl oz	$1^3/4$ cups
500 ml	16 fl oz	2 cups
625 ml	20 fl oz (1 pint)	$2^1/2$ cups
750 ml	24 fl oz ($1^1/5$ pints)	3 cups
1 litre	32 fl oz ($1^3/5$ pints)	4 cups
1.25 litres	40 fl oz (2 pints)	5 cups
1.5 litres	48 fl oz ($2^2/5$ pints)	6 cups
2.5 litres	80 fl oz (4 pints)	10 cups

DRY MEASURES

Metric	Imperial
30 grams	1 ounce
45 grams	$1^1/2$ ounces
55 grams	2 ounces
70 grams	$2^1/2$ ounces
85 grams	3 ounces
100 grams	$3^1/2$ ounces
110 grams	4 ounces
125 grams	$4^1/2$ ounces
140 grams	5 ounces
280 grams	10 ounces
450 grams	16 ounces (1 pound)
500 grams	1 pound, $1^1/2$ ounces
700 grams	$1^1/2$ pounds
800 grams	$1^3/4$ pounds
1 kilogram	2 pounds, 3 ounces
1.5 kilograms	3 pounds, $4^1/2$ ounces
2 kilograms	4 pounds, 6 ounces

OVEN TEMPERATURE

	°C	°F	Gas Regulo
Very slow	120	250	1
Slow	150	300	2
Moderately slow	160	325	3
Moderate	180	350	4
Moderately hot	190/200	370/400	5/6
Hot	210/220	410/440	6/7
Very hot	230	450	8
Super hot	250/290	475/550	9/10

LENGTH

Metric	Imperial
0.5 cm	$1/4$ inch
1 cm	$1/2$ inch
1.5 cm	$3/4$ inch
2.5 cm	1 inch